ALLEN CARR
NO MORE
ASHTRAYS

The pocket guide to quitting smoking

700038930429

To Ian McLellan, Charles Cooper and the rest of the team at
Arcturus Publishing for their marvellous contribution to our
mission to cure the world of smoking. Their hard work, creativity
and dedication have helped achieve more than 13 million Allen
Carr's Easyway book sales worldwide, saving millions of lives.

Allen Carr & Robin Hayley

ARCTURUS

This edition published in 2012 by Arcturus Publishing Limited
26/27 Bickels Yard, 151–153 Bermondsey Street,
London SE1 3HA

ISBN: 978-1-84858-083-1
AD001795EN

Printed in the UK

INTRODUCTION

Most smokers are convinced that it's difficult to stop smoking. The problem, we're told, is the enormous amount of willpower it takes to resist the craving to light up.

Wouldn't it be marvellous then not to have this battle of wills, and to be able to stop easily? The wonderful news is that there is an easy way, a way by which any smoker can quit immediately and permanently.

You will not have to use willpower, suffer withdrawal pangs or need substitutes. You will not even gain weight.

I know you might find this difficult to accept, but it's true.

I've been proving it for over twenty years, not only with my books which have sold more than thirteen million copies, but also at my worldwide network of clinics.

Not surprisingly, I call my method Easyway. My name is Allen Carr, and I am regarded as the world's leading expert on helping smokers quit. I can help you by exposing the myths and illusions about smoking.

Once you see through them, you will be free forever.

This book will provide you with an inspiring companion and enable you to stop smoking – easily, painlessly and permanently. I am so confident of your success that, if you fail to stop smoking with this book, you can recover its cost, in the form of a discount, if you attend one of my clinics, which are listed at the end.

So let me be your guide to stopping smoking enjoyably, and becoming what every smoker wants to be: a happy non-smoker. Let this be the first day of an exciting adventure: the day you start preparing yourself to quit easily, immediately and permanently.

Firstly though, please do not attempt to stop or to cut down until I advise you to do so. Carry on smoking as normal until that point. You could spend a lifetime trying to break into a safe and still not succeed. But if you know the correct combination, it's easy.

The nicotine trap is the most subtle, ingenious confidence trick that Mother Nature and mankind have ever combined to set. This book contains the key – the correct combination to the safe – that will allow you to escape. All you have to do is to follow a few simple instructions.

A QUESTION OF CHOICE?

Ask yourself a question: when did you decide to be a smoker? I don't mean, 'When did you have your first-ever cigarette?', but when did you decide to smoke every day?

In fact you never did; no one chooses to poison themselves with toxic fumes. You just drifted into it, like every other smoker on the planet.

MAYBE TOMORROW

So when will you quit? After you've spent
£100,000 (the amount an average smoker
spends on cigarettes in a lifetime)? When
smoking has crippled your health?
When the time feels right?

MAYBE NEVER

How many years have you been smoking?
Do you ever wonder why it never seems
to be the right time to quit?

I HAVE MY REASONS

Smokers give various arguments for smoking.

Because it tastes good. (Do you eat it?)
For something to do with your hands.
(Try a biro.)
For oral satisfaction. (Use a dummy.)

SPECIAL CIGARETTES

We talk about our favourite cigarettes:
for example, the first one in the morning.
Isn't that the one that tastes the worst?

Or the one after a meal or with a drink, when
answering the phone or during stress? How
can an identical cigarette out of the same
packet be so different from the ones you
smoke at any other time?

9

DO YOU WISH YOUR CHILDREN SMOKED?

If the answer is no, it means that you wish you were a non-smoker too. So why aren't you?

Some say it's just a habit that they find difficult to break. But habits aren't hard to break. In the UK we are in the habit of driving on the left; if we go to France, we break the habit immediately without difficulty.

SO WHY DO SMOKERS CONTINUE TO SMOKE?

There are no good reasons for smoking.

It doesn't taste nice.
It doesn't make you feel good.
It doesn't help you to do anything.

Smokers smoke for one reason,
and one reason alone:

THEY ARE ADDICTED TO NICOTINE! THE
MOST POWERFUL DRUG IN THE WORLD!

ADDICTED? REALLY?

Nicotine is the most powerfully addictive drug known to mankind. Just one cigarette is enough to hook you.

It's also a powerful poison. The nicotine content of just one cigarette injected directly into a vein would kill you. This is why those first cigarettes make you feel dizzy and sick. You're poisoning yourself.

CIGARETTES CREATE A NEED

When the nicotine from the cigarette you just smoked leaves your body, it creates an empty, insecure feeling. Smokers recognize this feeling as 'needing a cigarette' or 'needing something to do with my hands'.

If you light another cigarette, the nicotine is replaced and the empty, insecure feeling immediately disappears. This is the feeling that smokers describe as satisfaction or pleasure. It's like wearing tight shoes just for the pleasure of removing them!

GETTING HOOKED

When you extinguish the next cigarette, the nicotine leaves your system again, the empty, insecure feeling returns and you begin to crave another... and another... and another.

Nicotine, the most addictive drug known to mankind, has hooked another victim.

THE LITTLE MONSTER

Imagine that empty, insecure feeling as being a little nicotine monster, like a tapeworm inside your body that feeds on nicotine.

The true reason that any smoker continues to smoke is to feed that little nicotine monster.

BUT YOU ARE GOING TO STARVE THE LITTLE MONSTER TO DEATH!

THE ILLUSION OF PLEASURE

The nicotine trap is ingenious because it works back to front. It's when you aren't smoking that you suffer the craving. The moment you light up, the craving goes.

Your brain is fooled into believing that smoking is giving you a genuine pleasure or crutch. In fact, all it's done is create the problem in the first place. It's like those crooks who steal your roof tiles in the night, then offer their services to replace them for you during the day.

CRAVING NORMALITY

When you smoke a cigarette and feel that
sense of relief, all you are really doing
is relieving the aggravation of the body
withdrawing from the previous cigarette.
You are only getting back to the state you
enjoyed all the time before you lit
your first-ever cigarette.

In fact, you're just trying to feel like a non-
smoker, who doesn't suffer the aggravation
in the first place.

FALLING FURTHER IN

When you learn to smoke, you are teaching
your body to become immune to a powerful
poison and you build up a tolerance to
the drug.

As your tolerance rises, the relief you get
from the drug falls. After a short time you find
that one cigarette only partially relieves the
empty feeling, so you start to smoke more and
more, falling deeper and deeper into the trap.

PANIC

Imagine a heroin addict and the terrible panic they feel when they have no heroin. The wonderful feeling of 'pleasure' they describe when they plunge the needle into a vein is just the relief of that awful panic.

Non-heroin addicts don't suffer that feeling of panic. Obviously heroin doesn't relieve the panic – IT CAUSES IT!

DEPRIVATION

Now think about the panic you feel when you don't have any cigarettes and you can't get to the shops. How far would you go in the middle of the night to make sure you were stocked up with a supply of cigarettes?

Non-smokers don't suffer any such feeling of panic, of needing a cigarette. Neither did you before you became addicted to nicotine.

WHY YOU SMOKE

The only reason you or any other smoker ever needs or wants a cigarette is to try to get rid of the symptoms of nicotine withdrawal.

The irony is, only smokers suffer from nicotine withdrawal. Non-smokers do not. So all you are trying to do whenever you light a cigarette is to feel like a non-smoker!

A LITTLE CRUTCH

Isn't it true that it's not so much that you enjoy inhaling poisonous fumes into your lungs, but that you feel you can't enjoy social occasions or cope with stress without cigarettes?

The insecurity and stress you feel on such occasions is only made worse by nicotine addiction.

WHAT'S TO ENJOY?

Smoking is only hard to quit if you believe you get some genuine pleasure or benefit from it.

Once you realize that not only does smoking destroy your health and wealth, but also your nerves and confidence, then you can actually enjoy the process of quitting IMMEDIATELY AND PERMANENTLY!

THERE'S NOTHING
TO FEAR

One of the fears about quitting smoking is that
the withdrawal pains will prove unbearable.

Although nicotine is the world's most
powerful drug, its power – the speed at
which it enters and leaves the body – is also
its weakness.

A MILD ITCH

The actual physical effect of withdrawal from nicotine is so slight that smokers are hard pressed to describe it. They certainly couldn't point to a part of their body and say, 'This is where it hurts.'

They only know the feeling as, 'I WANT A CIGARETTE!'

THAT HUNGRY FEELING

Nicotine withdrawal feels identical to a hunger for food. With both, you feel irritable and empty when unable to relieve the feeling, and confident, happy and relaxed once you satisfy it.

But smoking is the complete opposite of eating.

A BIG DIFFERENCE

Good food genuinely tastes good.
Tobacco tastes foul.
Food is survival. Tobacco is death.
Food genuinely satisfies hunger. Tobacco
creates the craving.

Eating is a genuine pleasure we can enjoy
throughout our lives.

Smoking is an illusion of pleasure, an ingenious
confidence trick, which enslaves us for life.

LOSING TOUCH
WITH REALITY

Most smokers can remember how foul the first cigarettes tasted and how hard they had to work to inhale. After a while, smokers become immune to the smell and foul taste of tobacco.

They start to convince themselves that it's doing them some good.

THE BIG MONSTER

From birth we are subjected to a massive daily bombardment telling us that cigarettes relieve boredom and stress and aid concentration and relaxation. In films, when someone is about to be executed, the last request is always for a cancer stick. A husband chain-smokes outside the maternity ward. When the baby is born, cigars are handed round in celebration.

This is the brainwashing, or the 'Big Monster' that lives in the mind, and it is the real reason we find it difficult to quit.

SMOKING CREATES
THE BIG MONSTER

The Big Monster doesn't affect us before we become hooked on nicotine, because the beautiful truth is that we were complete before we tried those first experimental cigarettes.

But once we smoke a cigarette and introduce nicotine into our bodies, the Little Monster confirms the brainwashing or, more accurately, fools our brains into believing it. If you believe that you can't enjoy life or handle stress without a cigarette, you will feel miserable and insecure without one.

GOING WITHOUT

Think of the Little Monster as an almost
imperceptible itch that you only partially and
temporarily relieve by lighting up.

Like tight shoes, the longer you suffer,
the greater the relief. This is why the
so-called 'special cigarettes' follow a period
of abstinence: after sleep, a meal or exercise,
for example.

THE MORNING ROUTINE

The first cigarette of the day – the one that makes us cough our lungs up – is ironically a favourite for many smokers. It's just because you've gone eight hours without nicotine.

When we awake we relieve a series of aggravations: our bladders, our thirst, etc. A non-smoker will relieve his hunger; a smoker is more likely to light a cigarette.

CONFUSED SIGNALS

Although the nagging empty feeling is indistinguishable from hunger, nicotine will not relieve hunger for food, nor vice versa. This is why I became a chain-smoker.

After that first cigarette of the day, I still had the empty feeling, which was a hunger for food. But to my confused brain it meant I needed another cigarette, and another.

THE TUG OF WAR OF FEAR

All smokers suffer from a tug of war in their minds.

On one side is fear: it's filthy and disgusting slavery, destroying their health and wealth.

On the other side, 'It's my friend, my pleasure, my crutch.'

FEAR OF SUCCESS

But there is no genuine pleasure or crutch
in smoking. This side is also founded on fear:
'How can I enjoy life or cope with life without
cigarettes?'

Both sets of fear at each end of the tug of war
are caused by nicotine.
Non-smokers don't suffer from either.

NEITHER WILL YOU ONCE YOU ARE FREE!

PART-TIME SMOKERS

Some smokers wish that they were casual smokers. But there is no such thing. With any permanent itch, the natural tendency is to scratch it more and more. And the tendency for smokers is to smoke more and more.

So why aren't all smokers chain-smokers? Because we naturally battle to cut down our intake of poison.

CUTTING DOWN

Quitting means just that: NO MORE CIGARETTES! Cutting down does not work, for two reasons:

1. The less you smoke, the less it affects your health and wealth and the less you desire to quit.

2. The longer you go before scratching the itch, the greater the illusion of pleasure or support and the greater your desire to continue smoking. It also creates an even greater feeling of deprivation at times when you cannot smoke.

WHY GO WITHOUT?

Some smokers boast, 'I CAN GO A WEEK WITHOUT SMOKING,' but if it is a genuine pleasure, why would you want to go without it for a week? And if it isn't, why smoke at all?

I can go for a week without carrots but I feel no need to boast about it. Perhaps I would boast if I'd had to discipline myself and feel deprived for a whole week.

WHY NOT GO THE
WHOLE WAY?

If you feel good about smoking fewer
cigarettes, just think how great it will feel
to be completely free!

WHY SMOKERS LIE

Smokers lie to themselves because they sense that they've fallen into a trap and feel stupid and weak-willed because they've failed to escape from it.

This is why they give phoney reasons to justify their stupidity. They do it in order to retain some semblance of self-respect. No way do they deceive non-smokers. They don't even deceive themselves.

HEAD IN THE SAND

The vast majority of cigarettes are smoked without thought. If every time you lit a cigarette, you had to be aware of the cost, the filth in your lungs and the fact that this might just be the one to trigger off lung cancer, even the illusion of enjoyment would go.

THE ILLUSION OF HARDSHIP

The only reason smokers find it hard to quit is because the two monsters have fooled them into believing that they are making a sacrifice.

They believe that they have to go through a transitional period of misery and that, even if they succeed, they will have to resist temptation for the rest of their lives.

STOPPERS AND STARTERS

This piece of brainwashing is reinforced by smokers who stop for ten years, then start again; or those who are still moping about how they miss cigarettes ten years after stopping.

These tortured souls perpetuate the misconception that stopping is hard.

MISERABLE FAILURES

There are also ex-smokers who tell you how great they feel and who, next time you see them, are puffing away again.

Worst of all is the misery of your own failed attempts to quit when using willpower. This adds to the brainwashing and puts you off even trying to quit.

THE WILLPOWER METHOD

When trying to quit by using willpower, the smoker forces himself into a feeling of deprivation, like the tantrum of a child deprived of its sweets.

He hopes that, if he has the willpower to resist the temptation to smoke for long enough, one day he will wake up and feel free.

A TEMPORARY HALT

The willpower method doesn't work, for the same reasons that cutting down doesn't work.

After a few days, the congestion goes, you have more money, you no longer despise yourself and you have that wonderful holier-than-thou feeling of no longer being a slave.

LOSING THE
WILL TO QUIT

All the reasons that made you decide to stop
are rapidly disappearing.

Meanwhile, the Little Monster hasn't had his
fix and the Big Monster in your brain is saying,
'I WANT A CIGARETTE!'

OBSESSION TAKES HOLD

Now you want a cigarette but aren't allowed
to have one. You start to feel even more
deprived and miserable.

Soon your whole life is dominated by the
misery of not being allowed to smoke.

THE DRUG WINS

You start searching for reasons to have just one cigarette and eventually you find one. Your addiction has kept you imprisoned.

The longer you have suffered the misery of feeling deprived, the greater the illusion of pleasure when you do finally light up.

YOU ARE NOT
WEAK-WILLED

IT'S NOT LACK OF WILLPOWER THAT
KEEPS US SMOKING – IT'S A CONFLICT
OF WILLS.

At our clinics we put this question to smokers
who think they are weak-willed: if you ran out
of cigarettes late at night, how far would you
walk for another packet?

50

HERE'S THE EVIDENCE

A smoker would swim the Channel for a packet. It takes a strong-willed person to block their mind to the terrible health risks and continue to smoke. It takes a strong-willed person to resist the massive social pressures that smokers are subjected to nowadays.

The main illusion about smoking is that it relieves stress. Dominant people tend to take on stressful situations and often think smoking will help them relax. It's not that they are weak-willed.

A WILFUL REFUSAL TO QUIT

You'll find that your acquaintances who are
still heavy smokers are strong-willed in
other ways.

To repeat: IT'S NOT LACK OF WILLPOWER
THAT KEEPS US SMOKING – IT'S A
CONFLICT OF WILLS.

We are about to remove this conflict of wills.

YOU'RE GIVING UP NOTHING

Easyway works by removing the confusion and misconceptions that make it difficult to quit. Smokers try to 'give up' smoking. This implies a genuine sacrifice.

For the reasons I have already explained, there is absolutely nothing to give up. There is no sacrifice. The reality is the complete opposite.

YOU HAVE NOTHING
TO LOSE

What are the advantages of being a smoker?

There aren't any.

I don't mean the disadvantages outweigh the advantages. I mean there is no pleasure or crutch whatsoever in smoking.

YOU HAVE EVERYTHING
TO GAIN

On the contrary, smoking destroys your
nerves and confidence and creates boredom,
restlessness and dissatisfaction.

When you become a happy non-smoker,
you realize that every aspect of life is better
without cigarettes.

CIGARETTES ARE YOUR WORST ENEMY

Far from smoking being your friend, it would be difficult to imagine a worse enemy. It's only fear that keeps us hooked.

This is the subtlety of the nicotine trap. It makes us fear life outside it, when, in fact, the danger lies within.

OPEN YOUR MIND

You might find my claims hard to believe and be tempted to stop reading or to abandon your attempt to quit. Please don't fall into that trap.

If you need some encouragement, take a look at the thousands of testimonials from former smokers on *allencarr.com*.

Keep an open mind, follow my instructions and you will discover the same beautiful freedom that they now enjoy.

AN ENJOYABLE PRACTICE?

Do heroin addicts enjoy injections? Do cocaine users enjoy snorting for snorting's sake? No, these are just the rather disgusting methods they use to administer those drugs.

SMOKERS DON'T ENJOY SMOKING

Smokers believe that there is an actual pleasure in smoking and that the health risks and expense are merely hazards that interfere with that pleasure.

If that were true, smokers would enjoy herbal cigarettes. They never do. Smoking is simply nicotine addiction.

ARE YOU WITH ME?

If you are not yet convinced that there is nothing to give up and that the pleasure or crutch from smoking is merely an ingenious confidence trick, it is essential that you stop reading at this stage.

Go back to the beginning and start again. Remember, I have nothing but good news for you, provided you follow my instructions.

PICKING YOUR MOMENT

SO, WHEN DO YOU BECOME A NON-SMOKER?

It is important that you reflect on this question. A typical answer is, 'When I stop thinking about smoking.' But how will you do that and when will that be?

WHY WAIT?

Another answer is, 'When I can enjoy a meal or answer the phone without craving a cigarette.'

How long will you have to wait for that?

Or, 'When I've quit for a year.'

Why a year? Why not longer? It's all so vague and indecisive.

REMOVE THE DESIRE

The real difference between a smoker and a non-smoker is not that the latter doesn't smoke but that he or she has no **desire** to smoke.

If you have no desire to smoke, there is no temptation to smoke and, therefore, no need for willpower to resist the temptation.

THE RIGHT FRAME OF MIND

What you are trying to achieve is a frame of mind, so that when you extinguish the final cigarette, instead of thinking, 'I'd love a cigarette,' or, 'When will I be free?' you say to yourself:

'YIPPEE! I'M FREE!
I DON'T NEED TO SMOKE.
I DON'T WANT TO SMOKE.
I'M ALREADY A NON-SMOKER!'

REMOVE ALL DOUBTS

By clearing up all the doubts and confusion before you extinguish the final cigarette, you will ensure that you are free from that moment onwards.

That means seeing through the myths that surround smoking and that make it seem hard to quit.

THE MYTH OF SPECIAL CIGARETTES

Realize that there is no such thing as special or occasional cigarettes.

Special cigarettes come after a period of abstinence, or during a special occasion that you have really been enjoying in spite of cigarettes.

All cigarettes are the same. They are a lifetime's chain of misery.

THE MYTH OF SACRIFICE

Realize that you are giving up absolutely
nothing.

On the contrary, you are making marvellous
positive gains.

FREEDOM FROM FEAR

When I smoked, I knew I was literally burning my hard-earned money and risking terrible diseases. The chain reaction was like a time-bomb ticking away inside my body.

The fear was never knowing the length of the fuse, hoping I would quit before it went off. It's great to be free of that fear and self-loathing, but there were even greater unexpected gains.

A NEW VITALITY

I knew the coughing and congestion were due to smoking, but I thought the lack of energy was due to old age. I struggled to get up in the morning and fell asleep each evening watching TV.

It's great to wake up full of energy, feeling that you've had a good night's rest, actually wanting to exercise and feeling young again.

THE JOY OF GOOD HEALTH

As a youth I enjoyed medicals, believing I was
indestructible. As a smoker I hated them.
I even hated visiting other people in hospitals.
The mere thought of chest X-rays
caused panic.

Now it's so great to feel strong again, able to
enjoy the good times and be fully equipped
to cope with the bad.

FREE FROM MISERY

It never occurred to me that I spent half my life feeling miserable because I wasn't allowed to smoke and the other half feeling miserable because I did.

IT'S SO LOVELY BEING FREE!

NO MORE SELF-DELUSION

All our lives the fear of quitting makes us block the bad effects of smoking out of our minds. It's like an ever-increasing black shadow hovering over our existence.

Strong people hate being controlled by anything. The greatest gain is to be free of this dark cloud and self-loathing. You should pity, rather than envy, smokers.

A NEW WORLD, A NEW LIFE

When I finally discovered Easyway, it was like waking from a nightmare, escaping from a gloomy world of fear and depression into a sunshine world of health, confidence and freedom.

I STILL CAN'T GET OVER THE EUPHORIA, AND NEITHER WILL YOU.

FOLLOW YOUR INSTINCTS

Every animal on this planet instinctively knows
the difference between food and poison.
We know that there is something evil and
unnatural about breathing lethal fumes into
our lungs.

To have to do it all day, every day because of
the influence of a subtle, sinister drug is not
only evil but incomprehensible.

AN EASY DECISION

It is easy to decide whether to spend the rest of your life as a smoker or a non-smoker. The greatest gain is to be free from the fear that is caused by the drug.

You never decided to become a smoker for life, but you fell into an ingenious trap that was designed to enslave you permanently.

NO REASON TO DELAY

If you're concerned that this is not the right time for you to quit because of stress or other plans, I can tell you that this is part of the ingenuity of the trap.

BE AWARE OF IT!
DON'T FALL FOR IT!

You will only escape if you make a positive effort to do so and the first step is to take the decision to make that attempt.

DECISION TIME

I want you to have the courage to take that decision now. I'm not asking you to smoke your final cigarette yet – I'll advise you when to do that. All I ask is that you make the decision to go for it.

If you have the courage to do this and follow my instructions to the letter, you will not only find it easy but enjoyable.

IGNORE YOUR FEARS

If you have a feeling of doom and gloom,
dismiss it now. You are about to achieve
something wonderful, something that every
smoker on the planet would love to achieve.

FREEDOM

YOU ARE NOW FREE!

Start right now with a feeling of excitement,
challenge and elation.

KNOW YOUR ENEMY

For a few days after quitting, the Little Monster will live on. You might be aware of a feeling of insecurity or just, 'I want a cigarette.'

This barely noticeable physical discomfort disappears after about five days. After three weeks, the drug's effects will be completely gone.

THERE IS NO PAIN

The actual physical symptoms of withdrawal from nicotine are so slight that they were never enough to wake you up at night during your life as a smoker.

Smokers don't wake up in a panic, even though they've gone eight hours without nicotine. Most smokers nowadays will leave the bedroom, and many go for long periods of time, before they light their first cigarette.

WAKING THE BIG MONSTER

The reason smokers don't crave cigarettes while they're asleep is because the Big Monster is asleep. Once you're awake, the almost imperceptible physical discomfort created by the Little Monster acts as a trigger for the Big Monster in your brain.

It is the Big Monster that creates the fear and panic.

RECOGNIZE THE SIGNS

For a few days after quitting, the Little
Monster will live on. You might be aware of a
feeling of insecurity, or just: 'I want a cigarette.'
That's when ex-smokers get confused and
miserable because they can't have a cigarette.
They believe they are being deprived of
a genuine pleasure or crutch.

But you know that is not the case, so don't
worry about it. Recognize it for what it is. Say
to yourself, 'It's what smokers feel throughout
their smoking lives and what keeps them
miserable, poor, lethargic, unhealthy slaves!'

ENJOY KILLING
THE MONSTER

Rejoice in the fact that you have already
escaped from the prison. Revel in the death
throes of the Little Monster!

REMOVE ANY
LINGERING DOUBTS

You become a non-smoker the moment you extinguish your final cigarette. But how do you know it is your final cigarette?

Simply by removing all doubts and uncertainty first.

A PASTIME FOR FOOLS

Would you take up a pastime which gave you no pleasure or advantages whatsoever, that cost you a fortune, shortened your life and made you feel nervous, lethargic, unclean, stupid, and miserable?

The biggest idiot on earth wouldn't!

Having made what you know to be the correct decision, never punish yourself by ever doubting it.

A WORTHLESS COMPANION

Isn't it true that it's not so much that we enjoy smoking cigarettes, but assumed we did because we were miserable without them?

When your car broke down in the pouring rain in the middle of nowhere, can you remember lighting up and thinking, 'I'm late for the most important appointment of my life, but who cares? I've got this gorgeous packet of cigarettes.'

Did they make you happy and cheerful?

A BLOW TO YOUR CONFIDENCE

People at our clinics often say, 'I can't answer
the phone without a cigarette.' But what's so
stressful about the phone? It's that little itch
that's causing the stress.

That's also why smokers find it difficult to
concentrate without first removing the
distraction. Non-smokers don't seem to suffer
from the problem.

A MIND-NUMBING EXPERIENCE

Does smoking relieve boredom?

Boredom is a frame of mind. Smoking is not a particularly mind-stretching activity. You can smoke a dozen while watching a film on TV without even realizing it.

Can you think of anything more boring than chain-smoking cigarette after cigarette, day in day out, for 33 years, as I once did? We smoke when bored because there is nothing to distract us from the itch.

STICK TO YOUR GUNS

NEVER DOUBT YOUR DECISION TO QUIT!

It's the uncertainty that makes quitting
difficult. Having made what you know to be
the correct decision, never punish yourself by
questioning that decision.

FORGET 'THE ONE CIGARETTE'

If you see one cigarette as a pleasure and allow yourself to mope for it, you'll see a million cigarettes that way.

You'll be miserable if you don't have one and miserable if you do.

POSITIVE THINKING

DON'T TRY NOT TO THINK ABOUT
CIGARETTES! It might seem an obvious move
to push all thoughts of cigarettes from your
mind, but this is the greatest mistake smokers
make when they try to quit. It creates a phobia.

Remember, something marvellous is happening.
It's what you are thinking that's important. If it's,
'I can't have one,' or, 'when will I be free?' you'll
be doubting your decision. Instead, whenever
smoking comes into your mind, always think,

'YIPPEE! I'M FREE! I'M A NON-SMOKER!'

A SPECIAL MOMENT

If you follow my instructions, after just a few days you'll have a MOMENT. It might come during a social or stressful situation, one of those times you thought you could never enjoy or handle without a cigarette.

You will suddenly realize that not only did you enjoy or handle it, but you never even thought about smoking. That's when you know you are free. I call this THE MOMENT OF REVELATION.

WHEN DOES THE MOMENT COME?

DON'T WAIT FOR THE MOMENT TO HAPPEN. Just carry on enjoying your life as a happy non-smoker.

If you try to force THE MOMENT OF REVELATION, it can create a block in your mind.

LIFE AFTER QUITTING

You become a non-smoker the moment you cut off the supply of nicotine. You become a permanent non-smoker the moment you decide you no longer have any need or desire to smoke.

Accept that you'll have good days and bad, just as smokers do, and TRUST YOURSELF TO HANDLE ANY STRESS.

PRESERVE YOUR
GENUINE PLEASURES

Avoid making any radical changes to your
lifestyle. Just because you've quit smoking,
it doesn't mean you should avoid friends
who smoke. If you do, you'll be miserable.
Remember, you aren't giving up living.

You aren't giving up anything. On the contrary,
as your energy levels and confidence quickly
improve, you'll find your capacity to enjoy life
and to handle stress will also improve.

EASY DOES IT

Another subtlety of the nicotine trap is that our slide down into the pit is so gradual that we aren't even aware of the increasing debilitation of our physical and mental health.

When we quit, the recovery is also gradual. For people who use the willpower method, this gradual recovery adds to their feelings of misery and deprivation, leaving them blinkered against the immense gains.

Using my method, you can enjoy every moment of your physical recovery.

IT'S ALREADY HAPPENING

DON'T WAIT TO BECOME A NON-SMOKER! They say it takes seven years to clear the gunge out of your system, and that every cigarette you smoke takes five minutes off your life. Such statements are true, but only if you contract one of the killer diseases.

Quit now and your health will recover to almost 99 per cent of what it would have been if you'd never been a smoker, and the bulk of the gunge will leave in the first few days and weeks.

NOTHING STANDS IN YOUR WAY

Providing you remain on guard against further brainwashing, once you've cut off the supply of nicotine, nothing can prevent you from being free.

You will already be a non-smoker and it is essential that you think of yourself as one immediately. If you wait for it to happen, it will be like sowing seeds without watering them, then watching the ground in the hope they will grow.

ENJOY THE CHANGES

Any change for the better, such as a new job, house or car, involves a period of adjustment. You may feel somewhat strange at first, but the feeling will soon pass, provided you don't start worrying about it.

Remember, any slight aggravation you might suffer is not because you've quit smoking, but because you started in the first place.

TUNING OUT

DON'T WORRY IF YOU FORGET THAT YOU'VE STOPPED.

It's quite normal and a good sign. It means that already your mind isn't completely obsessed with smoking.

These are the times when willpower stoppers start to doubt and mope. Train yourself to reverse the moment immediately; remind yourself how lucky you are to be free.

Think, 'YIPPEE! I'M A NON-SMOKER!' and those moments become truly pleasurable.

PITY OTHER SMOKERS

NEVER ENVY SMOKERS. There is a constant battle between smokers and ex-smokers. As more and more smokers leave the sinking ship, those left behind feel more stupid, insecure, isolated and scared.

This fear can cause even people that love you to try to get you hooked again. Never forget that you hold all the aces and the smoker doesn't even have a pair of twos!

GET OUT THERE!

ATTEND SOCIAL FUNCTIONS
IMMEDIATELY. Even if you are surrounded by
smokers, always be aware that every one of
them would love to be like you: FREE.

They will expect you to be miserable. When
they see you happy and cheerful, they'll think
you are superhuman.

IT'S ABOUT HOW YOU FEEL

The important point is: YOU'LL FEEL LIKE
A SUPERSTAR!

ENJOY YOUR ESCAPE!

Revel in it.

THE DECISION IS YOURS

Remember, the Little Monster causes the physical itch, but it is only your brain that is capable of craving a cigarette.

For a few days the Little Monster might continue to trigger the thought, 'I want a cigarette.' Your brain has the choice of craving or recognizing the feeling for what it is…

...AND THINKING

'YIPPEE! I'M A NON-SMOKER!'

REJOICE FROM THE START

When a friend or a relative dies, you have to go through a period of mourning. Eventually, time partially heals the loss and life goes on.

When an enemy dies, you don't have to go through a mourning process. You can rejoice immediately and for the rest of your life.

NO FRIEND OF MINE

The cigarette was never a friend. It was the worst disease you'll ever suffer from. You can now take control.

You have the choice of spending the next few days moping over an illusion or rejoicing:

'YIPPEE! I'M A NON-SMOKER!'

REJECT ALL SUBSTITUTES

There are various cigarette substitutes on the market. Dismiss them. When you get over a bout of flu, do you go in search of another disease to take its place?

By even searching for a substitute you are perpetuating the belief that you are making a sacrifice by quitting.

FEEDING YOUR ADDICTION

If you substitute cigarettes with sweets or gum, or start picking between meals, not only will you get fat and miserable, but you won't relieve the very slight feelings of nicotine withdrawal anyway.

If you do find you put on a couple of pounds due to having a better appetite at main meals, there's no need to worry. When you've kicked smoking, you can control anything and you'll be able to lose that weight if you want to.

NICOTINE GUM AND PATCHES

The theory behind these substitutes is that, while you are breaking the habit, they ease the 'terrible physical withdrawal pains' and, when you've 'broken the habit', you wean yourself off the nicotine substitute.

But smoking is not a habit, it's an addiction. And the physical feeling of withdrawal is not terrible, it is almost imperceptible. Nicotine gum and patches only keep the Little Monster alive and keep the Big Monster craving!

ENJOY NOT SMOKING

If you can't visualize certain activities without smoking, break the association right now.

Have your drink, do your crossword, whatever you like to do. Enjoy doing them without smoking. Take satisfaction not only from removing the gunge from your body, but also from proving that smoking plays no part in the things you like to do.

YOU, THE NON-SMOKER

It's only smokers who can't enjoy life without nicotine. Soon you'll find it difficult to understand why you ever felt the need to smoke. You'll wonder why you can't make other smokers appreciate just how nice it is to be free!

SEE WHAT YOU'VE
ESCAPED FROM

OBSERVE SMOKERS AT SOCIAL
GATHERINGS. They almost all chain-smoke.
Notice how agitated they are when not
smoking. Watch the obvious relief when they
light up.

Observe how quickly the cigarette burns
and watch the increasing agitation when
the nicotine leaves their system. Remember,
tomorrow they have to continue the chain for
the rest of their lives.

REMIND YOURSELF
OF THE MISERY

OBSERVE SMOKERS GENERALLY. Watch
young girls smoking in the street, drivers in a
traffic jam, employees outside offices, holiday-
makers whose flights have been delayed or
lone smokers at parties.

Notice how smokers often don't even
seem to be aware that they are smoking,
how miserable they look and how even more
miserable they are when not allowed
to smoke.

READY TO QUIT

DON'T PUT OFF THE DAY.

The natural tendency is to pick a period
when you feel you least need a cigarette. Like
practically every other aspect of smoking, the
correct course is the complete opposite.

Prove to yourself straight away that you can
enjoy social occasions and handle stress.
The rest is easy.

DO IT NOW!

With a disease that gets worse and worse, it doesn't take a Sherlock Holmes to deduce that the quicker you get rid of it, the better.

If you had another disease and there was a simple cure, would you delay a single day? Smoking is the No. 1 killer disease in society. Fortunately there is a simple cure.

QUIT SMOKING NOW!

ANY REMAINING DOUBTS?

You should now be like a dog straining at the leash to smoke that final cigarette. If not, there can only be two reasons:

1. You do not believe that smoking provides no advantages whatsoever.
If so, read this book again from the beginning.

2. You do believe this, but still have a feeling of doom and gloom.
In which case, stop hesitating and trust me.

THE FINAL CIGARETTE

I want you to smoke your final cigarette
NOW. As you smoke it, do so not with a
feeling of doom and gloom, but with a feeling
of elation.

Now throw away your cigarettes and never
again keep cigarettes on you. You no longer
need them.

REJOICE

Just think how great the Count of Monte Cristo felt when he finally escaped from that prison.

Don't extinguish that final cigarette thinking, 'I must never smoke again.'

Think, 'ISN'T IT MARVELLOUS! I DON'T EVER NEED TO DO THIS AGAIN.'

NEVER ENVY SMOKERS

You are not being deprived. If you see someone smoking, no matter what the occasion, be aware that they are not smoking because they choose to.

They are being deprived of their money, health, energy, relaxation, self-respect and freedom. All that, and what do they achieve? Nothing! They are just trying to get back where they started and feel like a non-smoker again.

Smokers are all drug addicts and, as with all drug addiction, it'll just get worse and worse. Rather than envy them, PITY THEM.

Most important of all,
ENJOY THE REST OF YOUR LIFE AS
A HAPPY NON-SMOKER!

CONGRATULATIONS

You are now a non-smoker!

You have discovered how easy it is to
quit using Easyway. Simply by following
my instructions, you have made the most
important change of your life.

If you ever need to remind yourself of the key
points, I have listed them over the next three
pages. They will provide you with all the tips
you need for a happy, healthy life,

FREE FROM SMOKING

KEY POINTS

Remove all doubt. It's the uncertainty that makes it difficult to quit.

Rejoice right from the start. If you mope for cigarettes, you'll be miserable if you don't have one, and miserable if you do.

When smoking enters your mind, embrace it and think, 'Yippee! I'm a non-smoker!'

Don't wait for the moment of revelation. You'll know when it happens.

Handle stress. Accept that you'll have bad days just as smokers do, and remember that you're better able to deal with stress as a non-smoker.

You are already a non-smoker as soon as you put out your final cigarette.

Enjoy the changes you feel. You will soon grow accustomed to life as a happy non-smoker.

Be happy if you forget that you've stopped. It means that cigarettes are beginning to lose their hold over your mind.

Pity smokers. There is no reason to envy them. They wish they could be like you – FREE!

Attend social functions immediately. Every smoker would love to be like you. They will expect you to be miserable. When they see you happy and cheerful, they'll think you are superhuman.

Have no fear of nicotine withdrawal. The physical feeling is almost imperceptible and goes after a few days. When you feel the Little Monster craving, enjoy starving it to death.

Enjoy your freedom. When an enemy dies, you can rejoice immediately and for the rest of your life. The cigarette was never a friend.

Avoid all substitutes. They only perpetuate the belief that you are making a sacrifice by quitting.

Enjoy not smoking. Take pleasure in proving that you can enjoy all the same things you enjoyed before, without cigarettes.

Observe smokers. Don't avoid them, take heed of their strange and unfortunate behaviour. That used to be you. Isn't it great that you're free!

Forget 'just having the one'. There is no such thing. One cigarette leads to a lifetime's chain of filth, disease and misery.

Remember the trap. Just because you've quit easily, that doesn't mean you can smoke any time you like and just quit again. There is no good reason for any cigarette.

There is no genuine pleasure in smoking. It's like wearing tight shoes just for the relief of taking them off.

Smoking is not a crutch. The only stress that a cigarette is capable of relieving is the stress that the last cigarette caused.

You are not giving anything up. Cigarettes did absolutely nothing for you at all. So dismiss any feelings of doom or gloom and replace them with a marvellous feeling of excitement that the whole filthy nightmare is finally over and you are now free.

ALLEN CARR CONTACT INFORMATION

Worldwide Head Office and London Clinic: Park House,
14 Pepys Road, Raynes Park, London SW20 8NH
Tel: +44 (0)20 8944 7761 Fax: +44 (0)20 8944 8619
Email: **mail@allencarr.com** Web: **www.allencarr.com**

The following list gives details for Allen Carr's Easyway to Stop
Smoking Clinics in the UK where we guarantee that you will
stop smoking – or your money back. To find your nearest Allen
Carr's Easyway to Stop Smoking Clinic please call the
Central Booking Line (freephone)
on 0800 389 2115, email **mail@allencarr.com**
or visit **www.allencarr.com** and click '**Clinics**'.

Aylesbury	London
Belfast	Manchester
Birmingham	Milton Keynes
Bournemouth	Newcastle/North East
Brighton	Northampton
Bristol	Nottingham
Cambridge	Oxford
Cardiff	Peterborough
Coventry	Reading
Crewe	Scotland (Glasgow
Cumbria	and Edinburgh)
Derby	Sheffield
Exeter	Shrewsbury
Guernsey	Southampton
High Wycombe	Southport
Isle of Man	Staines/Heathrow
Jersey	Surrey
Kent	Stevenage
Leeds	Stoke
Leicester	Swindon
Liverpool	Telford

Worldwide Clinics

Allen Carr's international clinics extend across the globe to all
the countries listed below. Check for your nearest clinics by
visiting **www.allencarr.com** and clicking on '**Clinics**'.

Argentina	Italy
Australia	Japan
Austria	Latvia
Belgium	Lithuania
Brazil	Mauritius
Bulgaria	Mexico
Canada	Netherlands
Chile	New Zealand
Colombia	Norway
Cyprus	Peru
Denmark	Poland
Ecuador	Portugal
Estonia	Romania
Finland	Russia
France	Serbia
Germany	Singapore
Greece	Slovenia
Hong Kong	South Africa
Hungary	Spain
Iceland	Sweden
India	Switzerland
Ireland, Republic of (Dublin	Turkey
and Cork)	Ukraine
Israel	USA

OTHER ALLEN CARR BOOKS INCLUDE:

Allen Carr's Stop Smoking Now
ISBN: 978-184837-373-0

Allen Carr's Easy Way to Stop Smoking Kit (with 2 x audio CDs)
ISBN: 978-1-84837-498-0

Allen Carr's Illustrated Easyway to Stop Smoking
ISBN: 978-1-84837-930-5

Allen Carr's How to Be a Happy Non-Smoker
ISBN: 978-0-572-03163-3

Allen Carr's Smoking Sucks
(Parent Guide with 16-page pull-out comic)
ISBN: 978-0-572-03320-0

Allen Carr's Easy Way for Women to Stop Smoking
ISBN: 978-1-84837-464-5

Allen Carr's Illustrated Easyway for Women to Stop Smoking
ISBN: 978-0-572-03398-9

Allen Carr's Lose Weight Now
ISBN: 978-1-84837-720-2

Allen Carr's No More Diets
ISBN: 978-1-84837-554-3

Allen Carr's Easy Way to Control Alcohol
ISBN: 978-1-84837-465-2

Allen Carr's No More Hangovers
ISBN: 978-1-84837-555-0

Allen Carr's No More Worrying
ISBN: 978-1-84837-826-1

Available from all good book retailers